THE
COURAGE
TO
PARENT

Finding Our Strength . . . Empowering Our Children

JAN CLONINGER &
ROSEMARY STREMBICKI, LCSW

To Beth ?
Tracy —
Your girls are
blessed to have
such great parents!
(and grandparents)

"This book is designed to provide accurate and authoritative information in regard to the subject matter covered, and every effort has been made to ensure that it is correct and complete. However, neither the publisher nor the authors are engaged in rendering professional advice or services to the individual reader, and this book is not intended as a substitute for advice from a trained counselor, therapist, or other similar professional. If you require such advice of other expert assistance, you should seek the services of a competent professional in the appropriate specialty."

To Alex, Kate, and Emily Rose...

for your inspiration and lessons in parenting.

THE COURAGE TO PARENT

Contents

Introduction

Being a parent is one of the toughest yet most important jobs we do. We're required to gain new skills, seek out information, develop tools, and find support to do a job that few of us are ever really prepared for.

When I was pregnant with my son, I interviewed several pediatricians. The one I ultimately chose was on his third generation of patients. When I asked him about books I should read to get ready for parenting my son, he recommended the classic book Children: the Challenge. *The title says it all, and I can't tell you how many times I've uttered those words to myself when I felt frustrated or at a loss for what to do.*

There is no one perfect way to parent. Each family has to establish what works for it based on family history, cultural traditions, personal expectations, and the temperaments of the parents and kids.

There are, however, processes to consider, skills to develop and integrate into family life, and a commitment to be made to be present and intentional along the way.

When I first became a parent, I was a different person than I am now. When my son was five, our family experienced an unexpected event that forever changed our lives. It was painful and scary, and it caused everything I thought I knew about life to be questioned, examined, and turned upside down. The particulars of the event aren't important. Most of us have major challenges come our way at some point in life, but the process it called me to is what really changed everything.

I look back on that now and am grateful it happened (not that I'd ever want to go through something like it again!). It forced me to take a hard look at who I was and how I wanted to live my life from that point forward. The answers I found also changed the way I parented. I am convinced that had I not done that self-discovery work and made the resulting changes to my life, my son would not have grown up to be the incredible young man he is today.

It's why I am passionate about the process of living intentionally and authentically. I want you to know who you are and then attempt to create a life and family that reflects what you have found. It's also why I know that sometimes you need to have courage to continue on the path that is right for you.

Jan

"I had no idea parenting would be so hard." It's a refrain I hear over and over from parents old and new, who are facing a crisis or challenge in the everyday lives of their families.

Everyone faces parenthood with dreams, fantasies, and an overwhelming love like we've never before experienced. Along with the overwhelming love, however, comes an overwhelming feeling of responsibility. This sometimes borders on fear that we may not be up for the job. The reality is that we are up for the job, and if we parent with intention and explore our feelings and motivations, we can conquer that fear.

When my children were born, I had the luxury of living near a large, extended family, and all I had to do was reach out to a trusted family member when I lost my ability to cope, but a new job opportunity moved us a thousand miles away. I was left with few resources to call upon when I needed help with my one- and three-year-old. Luckily we moved into a neighborhood filled with young families, and we relied on each other for information, insight, and last-minute babysitting.

But our culture has changed in the past thirty years, many parents work all day, live away from family, and have little time to sit, chat, and problem-solve with other parents. How often do any of us have the opportunity to spend time undistracted with family and friends?

From the time I was a young child I've had an interest in the parent/child relationship. observing and trying to make sense of the impact they had on each other. That interest has become a passion, and through reading, education, and working with families, I've learned there is no definitive formula for raising successful adults. I have also learned that self-knowledge, positive intentions, and awareness are necessary throughout the process. And the key to meeting the challenge is the courage to reflect, ask questions, and meet our children where they are developmentally and temperamentally in order to guide them into adulthood.

So, here we are, working together to help our children identify and realize their hopes and dreams on the road to adulthood. I hope you find this book helpful in that journey.

Rosemary

The Parent Handbook

When my son was about eight, it became time to add an extra bath to his schedule each week. It didn't seem like too much to ask, but Alex was a master negotiator from the time he was born. Not being particularly fond of baths in the first place, he was not happy with this new development and decided to take a stand. He saw no reason to increase his bathing schedule and wanted some kind of outside authority to prove it was necessary to make the change. His dad and I gave all the basic explanations why, but we were continually met with resistance. Finally I said, "Because the *parent handbook* says at age eight your child has to put an extra bath into his weekly schedule!" It took Alex by surprise, and he demanded to see this parent handbook, to which I replied, "Sorry, you can't see it until you're a parent."

Alex wanted to know where we kept it, what else it said, and how he could trust us that it even existed. I promised him that when he became a parent someday he'd receive his very own copy. To my surprise, it worked. It then became a running joke. "Sorry, but it's in the parent handbook" was our initial response when he wasn't happy with one of our decisions. Ever since then, I've known that someday I would have to create a parent handbook to give him when he was about to become a dad.

I always envisioned printing him a book with lots of blank pages to fill out and just three simple phrases: know yourself, know your child, and love your child unconditionally.

I hadn't thought about the parent handbook for quite some time, but after reviewing the first draft of this book, I realized — *THIS IS* the parent handbook I have always wanted to pass on to him.

Granted, there are a few more words, but all these years later, the sentiment is still the same.

Jan

Each family is a unique blend of beliefs, values, culture, tradition, and histories. What works for one family may not work for another, but as parents, it's up to each of us to explore and discover the parenting path that works best for us.

Our philosophy is that, more often than not, you instinctively know what's best for you and your child, but with all the conflicting studies, opinions posted on the Internet, well-meaning input from family and friends, and your children trying to convince you they know better (especially as they move into adolescence!), it's easy to feel overwhelmed and have your confidence shaken.

It takes courage to parent. It takes courage to look inside yourself, honor and accept your children for who they are, change and grow as a person and a parent, and on some days, do what you know is right, even when your child isn't happy about it.

Each chapter of this book provides an opportunity to think about and capture answers that are relevant and important to your parenting process. And, the most exciting news is once you've done them all, you will have completed your very own parent handbook that will guide your parenting process!

It won't be so specific as to tell you how many baths your child needs each week, but it will serve as a reminder of who you are, what's important to you in life and as a parent, and the family history (both good and bad) you bring to the parenting process. It will provide an opportunity to develop a parenting plan, time to think about what makes your child unique, and ways you can best support your child in becoming his or her best self.

This book allows you to take proactive steps to help ensure your children have the best possible chance at becoming responsible, productive adults. It will support you in helping your children become resilient people who know themselves, interact well with others, set a course for their lives, live with a sense of purpose, move forward, and contribute to society.

To get the most from this book, we suggest you read each chapter and complete the questions before moving to the next. Even if it takes a few days or weeks, attempt to do each exercise before you move forward. What you discover in each chapter informs the next. Some of you may find it helpful to work through the exercises in a group setting. This way you can share your thoughts and find some accountability in completing the book.

- You can simply read the chapters without completing the exercises, and you will gain knowledge of the concepts presented, but by completing the exercises, you will better understand how the practical application will benefit both you and your family. Reading the book without doing the exercises may make you feel a bit overwhelmed, as it is designed as a process for the reader to engage with. It is not just a passing on of information.

- While you can take notes or respond to questions by writing in the book, we suggest you use a notebook, journal, or computer document to fully complete the exercises. Many of the questions require more space than provided, and what you create will become your personal parent handbook! As you revisit your handbook periodically, you can see what's changed and what's stayed the same and adapt it accordingly. In addition, if you have more than one child, when you get to the sections focused on your child, you'll need to fill out a separate exercise for each one.

- This book is also designed to work through with your co-parent(s). We use that term throughout the book because families come in all shapes and sizes. Your co-parent(s) may be your spouse, your partner, your live-in boyfriend/girlfriend, your ex, caregivers, teachers, and/or members of your family who regularly participate in the raising of your child. Whether married or single, you may have a network of people in your life who help parent your child, and it's important that, as much as possible, everyone is on the same page.

- Think about who is helping raise your child. We suggest you ask those most involved with the process to work through the book with you so you can compare answers. This will help you discover more about each other and start dialogues about yourselves, your relationships, and the parenting process you share. In this way assumptions, misunderstandings, and possible conflicts can be discussed and resolved before they become serious issues.

- If you are on your own with little or no support, when you get to the sections which suggest you compare answers with your co-parent, skip over those exercises, or consider how others who are important in your life may answer those questions. Perhaps you have a mentor, past teacher, friend, or relative who would be willing to discuss your answers so you can get feedback from another person.

- If you and your co-parent are both actively parenting your child but are unable to agree on a parenting plan, especially if you're not living as a family unit, consider the values most important to you in your parenting process and find the courage to be consistent. As your children grow you can remind them that the rules and expectations may be different between their parents, but they are expected to comply with you when you are together. As they grow older they will see the consequences of each parent's choices and have an opportunity to choose which set of values work best for them.

- If your children are old enough, you can also talk with them about the exercises in the book. Ask them to answer some of the questions to see what they say and/or reveal about themselves. Create conversations around the answers you've given to see if you are reading your children correctly, or to share stories about yourself and your past.

- You may find some of the questions aren't applicable to your experience. Perhaps you don't have extended family to consider or a religious community you're a part of. Perhaps you're not yet a parent, or your child is too little to determine what makes him/her unique. If that is the case, simply skip over those questions, and feel free to add questions we haven't addressed. The point of this book is to help create the parent handbook that will help guide you.

This book introduces many vital parenting considerations. If we explored each thought or even each chapter to the fullest, the book would be so thick no one could pick it up, and they wouldn't want to! So at the end of the book we have listed some resources and titles you can explore if you want to go deeper into any of the topics we discuss.

As a parent there may be times when you feel totally overwhelmed. Children's actions may become out of control, and you or your child may have desperate feelings that can lead to harm. If you struggle with those thoughts or feelings frequently, it is time to seek help from a professional (i.e., social worker, counselor, psychologist, and/or psychiatrist). Talk to a trusted friend, relative, or medical doctor about referrals to someone helpful, and make the call. It takes courage to seek help.

We have also founded *A Place To Turn To*, a nonprofit organization that offers parenting coaches who work one-on-one with families and provide group classes on many of the topics discussed in this book. In fact, if you get stuck or want someone to help you through any or all of the chapters in this book, you may want to consider working with a parenting coach.

A Place To Turn To also sends out monthly Parenting Reflections via e-mail. These reflections are designed to help you spend a few minutes each month thinking about your parenting process so you are consistently intentional along the way. If you'd like to be on that e-mail list, just let us know.

A portion of all proceeds from this book will go to support *A Place To Turn To* and its work. For more information visit our website: www. APlaceToTurnTo.org.

CHAPTER 1

Why Courage Is Vital to the Parenting Process

Being a parent is the one job we do that we don't know if we're doing it right for about twenty to twenty-five years!

It's not until our children successfully transition into adulthood that we can sit back and enjoy the fruits of our labor, seeing what incredible young people we have had the honor of raising.

It takes courage in the form of bravery, guts, nerve, valor, daring, and audacity to stay the course at many times along the way.

> **It takes courage to be a parent — because there are new challenges and possibilities each day.**

You may think a parent handbook would be filled with specific tips and tricks to guarantee your children will be great kids, but as we said in the introduction, what works with one family may not work with another. Simply following a prescribed set of parenting rules that someone else has created doesn't guarantee parenting success.

In reality the best advantage you can give your children is to be the best person you can be, which starts with knowing who you are and then living a life that reflects what you have found. In doing so you can develop a parenting plan that works for you and your family. One you can feel good about and be more consistent in following. With self-knowledge we gain confidence, and with confidence we gain the strength and courage to stay the course throughout the parenting process.

It's important to do the hard work as soon as possible. This includes knowing who you are, being on the same page as your co-parent(s), demonstrating your beliefs and values in your actions, setting and maintaining healthy boundaries, and developing and teaching your child strong emotional skills. The earlier we start the process in our lives and the lives of our children, the better. It will make the parenting process easier as they get older.

If we take the easy way out when our kids are younger by not doing the above work, throwing up our hands, thinking we'll just deal with it later, or not helping our children with the process of self-discovery and development, then our jobs will be much (often much, much) harder as our children move through the elementary and adolescent years.

Parenting is one of the most important jobs we ever do. Yet it is often something we spend little time thinking about until issues develop or problems arise. This book gives you an opportunity to be proactive in the parenting process, develop a parenting plan, and update it on a regular basis. This way you're much less likely to be caught off guard as your child continues to develop and grow.

When you come upon defining moments in your life and the lives of your children, it's important to summon the courage from deep within so those opportunities can become real moments of truth. It's up to you to find the strength to stand strong. Your example will help to empower your children as they face tough and important decisions in their lives. This is especially true at the moments when you:

- are called to stand by your values

- question yourself and your parenting skills

- don't match up with your partner's ideas or parenting style

- realize your child is different than you

- have to learn something new

- face ongoing change

- discover things aren't going as planned

- know it's time to let go

- see your child taking a different path than what you had planned

It takes courage to be a parent.

Chapter One of My Parent Handbook—
The Courage to Parent

Getting Started

Take a few minutes to think about what format (journal, notebook, Word document, etc.) you will use to create your parent handbook, and gather your materials.

As your first entry, write a dedication to remind yourself why reading and working through this book is important to you.

CHAPTER 2

Intentional Parenting and
Being a Positive Role Model

Parenting is much harder today than in generations past. It's not that there is something wrong with us or that the generations before us knew something we don't. Society is changing at a rapid pace, making it difficult and sometimes overwhelming to keep up.

Think about when you were a child. How has the world changed since you were growing up? Think about your parents' generation. How has the world shifted since they were kids?

Life used to be much slower paced. Just a generation or two ago, forty-hour work weeks were the norm. Families gathered around the dinner table most nights. Stores were closed on Sundays so people had downtime each week. There were a limited amount of television stations, so there were times when there was nothing to watch. There were no DVRs, video games, or expensive electronic devices, so people had to find creative ways to entertain themselves. During the summers children went out to play with the only restriction being they had to be home by dinner. Going to college (and finding the money to pay those costs) wasn't an automatic rite of passage. Kids grew up, rarely moved to another city, and had the support and resources of their families nearby. Young people started jobs, had opportunities to work their way up the ladder, and looked forward to retirement knowing the company would supply a great pension and health benefits they could rely on as they aged.

Now there's new technology, a new economy, globalization, and relocation. There's a lack of job security, job specialization that requires special education to get ahead, and little or no retirement benefits. Kids have more pressure to succeed in school and develop stellar résumés filled with extracurricular activities. There's more testing, select sports teams, and pressure to achieve an idealized physical appearance for both our girls and boys. There's a disconnection from extended family, complicated blended family issues, and kids shows where kids rule, and parents seemingly don't exist. There are twenty-four-hour news cycles, cable TV stations devoted to a myriad of topics and views, reality TV, the Internet, Facebook, Twitter, YouTube, cell phones, texting, sexting, bullying, and cyberbullying. There's increased exposure to sexuality at earlier ages, more zero tolerance policies, more fear, and more stress. There's less respect, downtime, family time, unstructured time, creative playtime, and time to be a kid.

Life has gotten more complicated, and being a parent today is tough. It's challenging enough just managing all the changes in our society and our own lives! Add in all the responsibilities, obligations, hopes, and dreams that come with being a parent, and it's no wonder so many of us are feeling overwhelmed or inadequate. So what's a parent to do?

Be intentional.

What do we mean by that?

Being intentional means you are awake, conscious, and aware of what's going on inside of you, around you, and in your parenting process.

Being aware of what's going on *inside of you* means you understand who you are and what makes you unique. You strive to live an authentic life. You understand your beliefs, values, and what's important to you, and your choices and behaviors are a direct reflection of what you've chosen. It means you can acknowledge and process your feelings in a responsible way. You have integrated, or are working on integrating, your past hurts and wounds so you're not carrying them with you daily. (This means you don't react inappropriately to current situations because of experiences you've had in your past.)

Being aware of what's going on *around you* means you understand the biases and baggage you might bring to a situation, but you know how to set those issues aside and focus on the reality of what's going on presently. It means you can pay attention to what's going on in the lives of those around you, and you can listen, be present, and be empathetic to them without being distracted by your own thoughts (or electronic gadgets!).

Being intentional in *your parenting process* means you have a clear definition of your role as a parent, you know what's important to your family, and you have an understanding of who your children are. (This includes their unique gifts, talents, and temperaments.) It means understanding how you can help your children become their best selves and grow into responsible, productive adults.

It also means you spend time thinking about how you parent, assess how well your parenting process is working, and adapt when necessary in order to support your children throughout their development and self-discovery process.

Our kids are always watching us, and what we do speaks louder than what we say to them along the way. The old adage "do as I say, not as I do" doesn't work anymore.

Children are also receiving messages from peers, the media, and society, so if you don't offer a clear and consistent voice, they will take their cues from those who are louder. Unfortunately this is often people they see in the media such as fame seekers, professional athletes, reality stars, actors, or the characters they play. While some of these people may be decent human beings, do we really want our children patterning themselves after people we don't really know? Wouldn't we prefer to be the ones who have a strong influence on our children's lives?

Think about people you admire in the world. What is it that attracts you to them? Do you admire them for what they've done, for who they are as people, or for how they live their lives?

We can all think of people who are great at sports but poor human beings in their day-to-day lives. There are also those that are well known in pop culture but have gotten famous because of their bad behavior. Then there are the people who have conquered the world of industry or finance but have lied, cheated, and hurt innocent people in order to get there. They may be famous or considered successful, but are those the kinds of people we want our children to aspire to be?

Often the best role models are those who live authentically. We may not completely agree with their beliefs or values or identify with what they feel is most important in life, but they're people we admire because what they do is a direct reflection of who they are. They are consistent, predictable, and dependable.

Think about the outstanding athlete that frequently gives back to the community, the person who has become well known and uses that celebrity to positively impact society, or the business person who is successful and uses that success to help others. Those are people who have decided that what they give is as important as what they get, and they order their lives accordingly.

Authentic people possess traits that cannot be attained through beauty products, possessions, fame, or celebrity. They aren't seeking external gratification or affirmation. They live from the inside out, knowing their personal opinion of themselves is what truly matters. They know their strengths and power, and self-acceptance comes from within. People who live authentically are attractive because they have the consistency, confidence, courage, and clarity we instinctively desire.

As parents we are not able to impose our beliefs and values on our children, but we can enhance the possibility of them embracing what's truly important to us if we model those behaviors consistently throughout their lives. As they see us making choices that reflect what's important to us, they learn how to be intentional and authentic themselves.

If we don't do that work, it can be difficult for our children to get a clear message of our personal and family values. If we send mixed messages or allow peers, the media, or celebrities to shape our children's principles, we can't be disappointed when they believe or act in ways that are counter to what we feel is important.

> **Children who aren't provided a clear and consistent role model often struggle with discovering and being consistent in their own values as they grow and transition into adulthood.**

If we haven't done the work of self-discovery and prioritizing our lives to reflect what's important to us, it's difficult, if not impossible, to guide our children through that discovery process.

Chapter Two of My Parent Handbook—
Being Intentional and a Role Model for My Child

Being Intentional

1. On a scale from one to ten (one being the lowest) how would you rate your ability to know what is going on inside of you (tuning in to your feelings, intuitive senses, inner messages, emotional baggage, etc.)?

2. What percentage of the time are you aware of what's going on inside you?

    - In your personal life?

    - In your professional life?

    - In relation to your child?

3. On a scale from one to ten, how would you rate your ability to know what is going on around you (tuning in to what's important, situations, other people, etc.) and letting go of unnecessary distractions?

THE COUR

4. What percentage of the time are you aware of
    going on around you?

    ▪   In your personal life?

    ▪   In your professional life?

    ▪   In relation to your child?

5. Rare is the person who is 100 percent intentional all
    the time. However, the first step in becoming more
    intentional is to be aware of its importance and practice
    to develop our strength. What do you need to learn in
    order to be more intentional? How might you practice
    being more intentional in the weeks ahead?

What Kind of Role Model Are You?

1. Who have been the role models in your life (positive
    and perhaps not so positive)? What have you learned
    from them?

2. Are you happy with the kind of role model you are for
    your children? As your children observe your behaviors

and the way you live your life, what positive aspects do they see?

3. As your children observe your behaviors and the way you live your life, what negative aspects do they see?

4. Are there areas where you'd like to be a stronger role model? What shifts could you make in your life that would help you set a better example for your children?

5. List the other people who have a strong presence in your child's life. Go back and think about what positive and/or negative aspects they model for your child?

Research shows that parents, more so than schools, teachers, or peers, still have the greatest influence on a child's capacity to succeed. While it sometimes seems as if kids are looking in all the wrong places for affirmation and role models on which to pattern their lives, your influence still matters most.

CHAPTER 3

What's Important to You

The demands of being a parent are varied and great. A shift of consciousness occurs the moment you discover you're going to have a child. Suddenly you are completely and totally responsible for someone other than yourself. In a few short months, a new life enters the world, and it is one that is completely helpless and totally dependent on you for everything. It can be overwhelming to experience so much love and responsibility for that new little person because, at the same time, you often feel so unprepared.

Throughout history new parents have been surrounded by extended family or communities who could model parenting skills. Often times these people helped pass down stories, examples, and traditions that helped new parents shape their children into responsible, productive members of society.

However, in today's world, families often aren't living in close proximity to one another. Support systems have disappeared. Parents feel isolated and on their own to figure out what moral and ethical boundaries they want to set for their children, and then they must find ways to make those lessons stick.

Many of us delve into books about how our children are developing in the womb and even more books about what to expect once they arrive. We seek out developmental milestones and look for the latest and best advice on what our children need. We then start searching

THE COURAGE TO PARENT

the Web and find conflicting information, unsupported opinions, and a myriad of products that suggest we can't raise our children without purchasing all of them.

It's confusing and unsettling, and it often creates a lot of unnecessary and unproductive anxiety because we feel like we don't know what we're doing. We feel we're not doing things right, and we live in fear that our child is going to grow up to be "one of those kids" that none of us want to claim as our own.

It's easy to have our confidence shaken and to stop listening and trusting our own instincts. We get so busy and overwhelmed that we forget the things that are important to us, and we start parenting based on other people's opinions, priorities, and expectations.

> **As a parent it's easy to lose ourselves along the way, put ourselves last, and forget what's truly important in life, especially if we weren't certain of those things as we began the parenting process.**

A vital step in the parenting process is to delve into discovering and affirming who we are as individuals, parents, and a budding family. This way we grow in our confidence, learn to trust our instincts, and develop greater clarity about what's important to us and our family as we live our lives.

So, what is important to you as an individual? As a parent? As a family? How will you measure your success as a parent as your child grows into adulthood?

Take a second to flash forward to the time when your child is thirty years old. How will you know you've done your job well?

Literally stop reading right now, and think about it. Consider writing down or making a list of what you envisioned. Once you have a clear picture, come back to this spot and keep reading.

What did you imagine?

Did you think about your children's careers, earning potential, or the houses they might live in? Did you envision their lifestyle, what they had attained, or the travels they had experienced?

Was your list focused on the kind of character you hoped they would have? Did you envision specific traits such as kindness, empathy, resiliency, self-knowledge, or inner strength?

Did your list contain a combination of all those things and more?

Often people focus more on the tangible accomplishments such as careers, possessions, and wealth. As a society we value what people do and what they have. In fact think about what happens when we meet someone new. Oftentimes the first question we ask after we learn someone's name is what that person does for a living. Have you ever caught yourself comparing your clothes, car, or status of living with someone you've met to see where you compare?

It's easy to get caught up in believing that jobs, money, and possessions can make us happy. Most agree, however, in the end it is knowing who you are, having good relationships, and living an authentic life (one that aligns our actions with what's most important to us) that makes us feel good about ourselves and brings us the greatest satisfaction.

Using the exercises at the end of this chapter, consider who you are by taking an inventory of your own:

- interests, gifts, and talents

- temperament and motivation

- beliefs and values

- cultural background and family history

- personal dreams and goals

Try not to let the number of questions in this chapter overwhelm you! Since knowing yourself is a foundational component of the parenting process, this chapter has the most questions. It will take longer to complete than the chapters that follow.

The process of self-discovery is different for all of us. For some it is a familiar exercise that guides our daily lives. For others it's new and may initially take more effort. For those who had a difficult childhood the process might even feel a bit daunting. As you become more familiar with personal reflection, though, you may be surprised at how quickly it becomes a source of understanding who you are, how you developed, and how you can become who you want to be.

Sometimes it helps to work through the process with an objective person. Friends, mentors, parenting coaches, and/or private therapists can offer resources if you feel stuck. Just be sure to do the work. It's a vital step in being intentional about your own life and the parenting process.

Chapter Three of My Parent Handbook —
What's Important to Me

Choose how to approach this chapter in a way that works best for you. There are several sections of open-ended and multiple-choice questions to help you think about and clarify what is important to you. There is also an opportunity to summarize what you know or discover at the end of the exercises in this chapter.

There are no right or wrong answers. This isn't a scientific study or psychological profile. It's an opportunity to get to know yourself better, capture and/or share what you've found, and set priorities when making decisions that shape you and your family's life.

My Personal Preferences

1. I enjoy spending my free time…

2. I chose my line of work because…

3. If given the choice of spending time alone, spending time with a small group of friends, or going to a big party, I prefer...

4. I tend to be:

   a. focused on the past

   b. in the present moment

   c. always looking toward the future

5. I consider myself:

   a. a big picture person

   b. someone who prefers to focus on how to take the next step

   c. somewhere in between

6. I make my decisions based on:

   a. logic

   b. my values

   c. emotion

   d. depends on the situation

7. When I'm frustrated or angry, I...

8. When I'm sad or scared, I...

9. If I could change one thing about myself, I would...

10. Which statement best describes you:

    a. Things must be neat and orderly.

    b. I like things neat and orderly.

    c. Sometimes neat and orderly is nice.

    d. I really don't care if things are neat or orderly.

11. I learn best by:

    a. watching or reading something

    b. listening (to a teacher talking or a lecture)

    c. participating or doing

12. If I won $10,000, I would...

13. My favorite color is…

14. Other than my child and/or co-parent, the most important person in the world to me is…

15. My most prized possession is…

16. My most cherished memory is…

17. If cost were not an issue, I would really like to visit…

18. I would like to have a conversation with (living or not)…

19. If time travel becomes a reality, I would like to travel to…

20. Three things on my bucket list are…

My Relationships with Others

1. When it comes to friends, I most appreciate...

2. My friends would say they like me because...

3. Which statement best describes you?

    a. I will avoid conflict at all costs.

    b. I am comfortable working through conflict.

4. What is your preference?

    a. I prefer to be with people who think like me.

    b. I welcome different points of views.

5. When working on a project:

    a. I prefer working alone.

    b. I like working with a partner.

    c. I like working with a team.

6. When it comes to friends:

    a. I enjoy having a big circle of friends, even if I don't know everyone personally.

    b. I prefer to have a few very close friends that I know well.

7. Thinking about my communication skills:

    a. I am confident in my ability to communicate my thoughts and feelings.

    b. It is difficult for me to share my innermost thoughts and feelings.

8. When it comes to your closest relationships:

    a. I want to be in charge.

    b. I like being equals.

    c. I prefer the other person is in charge.

9. When it comes to spending time with friends, I most enjoy…

10. If I could change one thing about my closest relationships, I would…

My Beliefs and Values

1. A few of my favorite quotes or sayings are...

2. Some of my favorite songs are...

3. Politically I would describe myself as...

4. To me religion...

5. Those that know me best know I believe...

6. My actions demonstrate that I...

7. My decisions are most often based on...

8. The people I admire most are (who and why)...

9. I would use the following words to describe the kind of person I am...

10. In the end what's most important to me is…

My Gifts, Talents, Passions, and Purpose

1. If I could change one thing in the world, I would…

2. I get excited when I think about…

3. I have always been interested in…

4. Friends, coworkers, etc., tell me I am good at…

5. I would like to learn to…

6. I am my happiest when I am…

7. I am comfortable saying I am very good at…

8. I would like to enhance my ability to…

9. I feel good about what I am doing when...

10. I am most motivated by...

11. For now I think my purpose in life is...

12. In ten years I see my life...

13. In twenty years I see my life...

14. My fondest hopes and dreams are...

15. I am taking these steps toward creating the life of my dreams...

My Family of Origin

1. Growing up my family's religious and/or cultural traditions included...

2. My family's rules were...

3. My parent(s) disciplined me by...

4. The spoken or unspoken family messages I received as a child were...

5. Growing up I saw my family had a pattern of...

6. My family:

    a. kept secrets

    b. was an open book

7. I consider my family to have been:

    a. healthy and a good example of how relationships should work

    b. dysfunctional and not an example of how relationships should work

8. When I reflect back on childhood, I feel...

My Family Now

1. With my children it is important I establish or carry on the following family, religious, and/or cultural traditions...

2. It's important my family has rules such as...

3. When it comes to disciplining my children, my philosophy is...

4. With my children it is important I carry on OR end family messages such as...

5. With my children it is important I carry on OR end family patterns such as...

6. When it comes to family secrets...

7. I would really like to see my child carry these three beliefs and/or values into adulthood...

8. When my children are grown, I hope they reflect back on their childhood and feel…

9. When I think about parenting, I will feel like a success if…

10. My greatest wish for my children is…

My Life Story

If you like, summarize all you've come to realize about who you are and what's important to you using the following exercise.

What is your life story? Without censoring yourself or editing as you go, write the story of your life in a few paragraphs. What are the themes, lessons, philosophies, hurts, victories, etc., that define who you are today?

It takes courage to look inside ourselves, discover what's truly important, and order our lives accordingly. The more we do the work for ourselves, the more equipped we will be to help our children with their process as they grow.

CHAPTER 4

Are You on the Same Page

_____

As we discussed in the last chapter, children need clear and consistent messages about what's important to us. We're rarely the only person in our children's lives, however, so we have to look at how the relationships with our co-parent(s), extended family, and community impact our parenting process. In order to be intentional, we also need to look at how those relationships can enhance or undermine the messages we want to send our kids.

Co-parents(s)

Parents may have different interests, temperaments, gifts/talents, and motivations. Unfortunately when parents' beliefs, values, and parenting philosophies aren't on the same page, children grow up receiving mixed messages. It makes it difficult for a child to distinguish what the rules are within the family context, and it can make it more difficult for them to read the social cues and rules of society at large.

After we consider who we are and what's important to us as parents, it is vitally important we compare our discoveries with our child's other parent (or anyone else helping fill that role).

It's rare to find people who line up exactly with our ideals. (Relationships wouldn't be as interesting and complex if they did!) It is important, however, to come to some mutual understanding on shared beliefs, values, and parenting philosophies when it comes to raising children together.

> **Just being aware of where there is common ground and where there are differences can create an opportunity for discussion, compromise, and the development of an agreed upon plan to avoid unnecessary conflict down the road.**

Our kids can understand their parents aren't carbon copies of each other, and they may not agree 100 percent on all things. In fact understanding and seeing that at play can help them understand their own uniqueness and develop more tolerance of people who might be different than them. On the issues that matter most about raising our children, though, it is important we present a united front. This holds true even if it means one parent deferring to the other on a particular issue because it's been discussed and agreed upon.

Growing up with mixed messages can be very confusing to children and hinder their development. If, for example, one parent believes money is a tool to be spent and enjoyed, and the other parent believes money equals security or is a measure of success and therefore should be saved, children can grow up conflicted about their ideas regarding money.

If one parent is committed to one set of religious beliefs and the other parent to a different set, children may have trouble deciding which beliefs to identify with, unless the parents teach their children to honor and create traditions that complement and respect both.

If one parent values education, and the other values sports, children may have difficulty following their own path while trying to please one or both of their parents.

Children who are raised with conflicting messages, both spoken and unspoken, can struggle long into adulthood to find consistency in their lives. Feelings of guilt or betrayal may arise if they choose one parent's choices over the other.

After you and your co-parent have completed the "what's important to me" exercises in the previous chapter, schedule time to sit down and compare answers. Then complete the "how well do you align with you parenting partner(s)" exercise together.

The additional exercises in this chapter should be done individually and then compared and discussed. Use these exercises as a tool to document where you agree and disagree, and propose ways to prioritize and compromise in a way that is satisfying.

At the end of the chapter there is an opportunity to create a parenting mission statement together which reflects what you both agree is important to the parenting process. Understand that these exercises and your final document will be reviewed and revised from time to time.

If it becomes difficult to find amicable solutions during this process, consider skipping ahead to chapter nine on active listening and emotional coaching, and try to integrate some of those skills into the process of working through this section with your co-parent(s).

Chapter Four of My Parent Handbook—
Parenting Together

How Well Do You Align with Your Parenting Partner(s)?

Review your responses to each of the exercises in the last chapter (listed below).

1. How do your responses to the previous chapter align with your parenting partner(s)? How/where do you find common ground in the answers you gave regarding:

    a. personal preferences

    b. relationships with others

    c. beliefs and values

    d. gifts, talents, passion, and purpose

    e. family of origin

    f. life story

    g. your family now

2. Are there differences that do or could cause conflict between you and your parenting partner(s)? How can you proactively work through those differences before they become issues?

Day-to-Day Parenting Philosophies

Answer the following questions separately, and then discuss your answers to see where you are on the same page and where some negotiations and/or new possibilities need to be explored.

1. What level of participation do each of you expect to have in the parenting process? In what ways do each of you prefer to be involved?

2. What are your expectations for childcare at the various stages of your child's life (e.g., a parent staying home, a professional childcare setting, a professional childcare provider in your home, a relative providing childcare, etc.)?

3. Should there be equal parenting (all responsibilities and chores shared) or a division of labor (each parent having certain parenting responsibilities and/or jobs)?

4. When it comes to parenting, what are your most important priorities?

5. When it comes to parenting, what is your definition of discipline?

6. What do you feel is the best way to discipline your children when they are a...

    a. toddler

    b. preschooler

    c. early elementary school child

    d. third through fifth grader

    e. middle school child

    f. high school student

7. If you are past some of the stages listed above, how well do you feel your philosophy of discipline has worked so far? Do you need to reevaluate your definition and/or philosophy of discipline?

8. What's your philosophy toward children participating in chores at your child's current and next stage of life?

9. Do you think allowances should be earned or freely given to your child? At what age do you think it should start?

10. What is your philosophy regarding spending money on your children?

   a. Do their needs take priority over everything else?

   b. Do you spend a percentage of your income or set up a budget for their expenses?

   c. Do you pay for basic needs but feel they're responsible for everything else?

   d. Will you buy them a car?

   e. Will you pay for their college?

11. Think about food and family meals. Do you have strong preferences for what your child eats or how meals are structured?

12. What are your expectations regarding manners and your child's behavior in public or at other people's houses?

13. What's appropriate playtime with your child now and in his or her next stage of life?

14. When it comes to electronics, how do you feel about video games, phones, Internet access, and social media at your child's current and next stage of life?

15. What's your philosophy regarding how to educate your child (home school, public school, religious school, or private school)? Overall, what are your priorities when it comes to your child's education?

16. What is your philosophy regarding sex education and adolescents engaging in sexual activity?

17. What is your philosophy regarding your child's alcohol, tobacco, and/or drug use as they go through adolescence?

18. Do you think it's appropriate for your child to get piercings or tattoos? At what age?

19. When thinking of your child and how you'll invest your time, energy, and resources, how do you rank the importance of the following? Do some have more

weight over others, or are they all equally important to you?

    a. education

    b. sports

    c. health

    d. recreational time

    e. popularity

    f. character

    g. creative pursuits

    h. family relationships

    i. extended family relationships

    j. honoring cultural heritage

    k. religious upbringing

20. How would you like to prioritize your time individually and as parents? Note, we all have the same 168 hours a week.

    a. work

    b. personal leisure

c. family time

d. couples time

e. recreational time (with or without the family)

While working on the above exercises can help you and your co-parent(s) determine your parenting philosophies, priorities, and preferences, it can also be helpful to talk about your parenting styles. Often parents have different approaches. This is usually modeled on the way they were raised or the exact opposite of how they were raised, depending on their childhood experiences. Parents don't necessarily need identical parenting styles, but it is helpful to be aware of the dynamics. Consistency and respect are the foundations on which to build a style that will allow your children to grow, make mistakes, and learn.

When there is a great difference in parenting styles it can leave children feeling confused or as if they must adopt different behaviors according to who they are with. This distracts from the child's ability to discover his/her true self. Children work hard to meet our expectations, and when expectations differ greatly it's hard for them to know and internalize what is "right."

Parenting styles can be characterized by three basic types: permissive, authoritarian, and balanced.

Parents with a permissive style usually have very few rules and little or no consequences in place. They tend to engage in endless negotiation with their children, and the leadership role in the family is not always clearly defined. (Everyone's opinion in the family has equal weight.) Permissive parents tend to be less involved with their children's choices, and their children often grow up feeling entitled and/or rebellious.

Authoritarian parents tend to have rigid rules that are strictly enforced. Negotiation rarely takes place, and it is clear they are the leaders and absolute authority in the household. Authoritarian parents tend to be very involved in their children's choices. Their children often grow up having difficulty making decisions since they haven't had the opportunity to develop those skills for themselves.

Parents who have a balanced approach have firm rules that are consistently enforced, but they are open to negotiation. They provide stable leadership and are available to help their children with their choices as needed. In a household with a balanced approach everyone's opinion is respected. These children often grow up feeling more confident.

Parenting Style

1. What parenting style were you raised with?

2. What is your preferred parenting style?

3. How does it compare with your co-parent(s)?

Extended family

It's also important to realize we might or might not be on the same page with members of our extended family. Again, each of us is a unique human being, and it's hard enough to be on the same page with just one other person let alone an entire family!

Intentionally sitting down and determining where there is agreement or potential issues in the near or not-so-near future can go a long way in establishing your nuclear family's rules and avoiding conflict down the road, especially if extended family members are going to play an ongoing, active role in your child's life through regular visits or in a caretaking capacity.

As you develop a clear picture of what's truly important in raising your children you will be able to articulate your parenting preferences to those around you. Knowing what's important to you and your co-parent(s) and presenting a united front will help you find the strength to set clear and consistent boundaries with your extended family and others.

If conflict does arise, remember that we're not in the business of changing our families. Knowing what the differences are and being able to explain those differences, though, will help our children see that different people make different choices, and the choices they make reflect who they are. It's a great opportunity to talk to our children about who they want to be.

We also want to offer a word of caution here. Each parent should deal with his or her own extended family when expressing rules and setting boundaries. Many misunderstandings, hurt feelings, and family rifts are started because an in-law tries to take on that role with a co-parent's family. Each parent should deal with his or her own family directly and as lovingly as possible, assuring them that, as co-parents, you are on the same page and support each other.

Remember, just because there may be differences of opinion it doesn't necessarily mean one person is right and another wrong. Sometimes there are simply differences, and you may need to agree to disagree. You have the right to choose what you will bring forward into your new family and what you will leave behind. This applies to both wonderful traditions and unhealthy patterns of behavior. It's up to you, as parents, to determine the legacy you are going to pass onto your kids.

Each parent has a distinct personal family history. Think about these questions individually, and then work together to determine how your extended families match up and/or bring different philosophies to your parenting experience.

Extended Family

1. Growing up, what was most important to your family:

    a. hard work

    b. leisure time

    c. community involvement

    d. strong character (doing the right thing)

    e. basic sustenance (putting food on the table)

    f. spending time with family

    g. education

    h. religion (spiritual development)

2. Reflect on your childhood memories and think about…

    a. positives you'd like to recreate for your children

    b. negatives you'd like to extinguish

3. When it comes to discipline, my family…

4. When it comes to money, my family…

5. When it comes to spending time together, my family…

6. How important is it your extended family approves of your parenting process?

7. How much of an influence will your extended family have on your children?

8. Does your extended family share your values and goals?

9. When I think about the following members of my family, what behaviors (both positive and negative) do they model for my children?

    a. my mother

    b. my father

    c. my brother(s)

    d. my sister(s)

    e. my grandmother(s)

    f. my grandfather(s)

    g. my aunt(s)

    h. my uncle(s)

    i. members of my blended family

    j. others

10. Are there potential problem areas that need to be discussed or healthy boundaries established?

Friends and greater community

There is often a broader circle of friends and community that are more than happy to weigh in on what should be important to us and how we should raise our kids! Taking the information we've worked through personally and as a couple, and in consideration of our extended family, we can also begin to assess where there are perfect matches and places where boundaries are needed. In this way we can find the strength to parent with the beliefs, values, cultural history, family history, dreams, and goals that are important to us.

Our Friends and Greater Community

1. When you think of the following groups of people with whom you're associated, for the most part, do they reflect your family's values?

    a. your group of friends

    b. your neighborhood

    c. school

    d. work

    e. religious community

2. Is it important to you that any of the following groups approve of your parenting process?

    a. your group of friends

    b. your neighborhood

    c. school

    d. work

    e. religious community

3. Do you need to set clear boundaries to limit any negative influences on your children from:

    a. your group of friends

    b. your neighborhood

    c. school

    d. work

    e. your religious community

Your Shared Beliefs, Values, and Parenting Philosophies

Once you and your co-parent(s) have completed the exercises in this chapter and compared and discussed your responses, spend some time writing a joint statement that reflects your shared beliefs, values, and parenting philosophies. Think of it as a parenting mission statement that will help guide your decisions and parenting process. (You can use any or all of the prompts below or create ones of your own.)

In order to best support our children in becoming responsible, productive adults…

We agree it is important…

During the parenting process, when differences arise…

We will support each other…

It is our hope…

It takes courage to stay true to who we are, find places to compromise without sacrificing what's important to us, accept those around us who believe or live differently, and be consistent in character, especially if others are trying to influence us.

When we find the sweet spot of living our lives in that way, we become powerful role models for our children. Not only are we clearly articulating our beliefs and values (hoping those values will become our children's someday), we are showing them how to find their strength and stay true to who they are no matter what friends, acquaintances, pop culture, or any other person tells them they ought to be.

Imagine how it would feel to know your children learned to live their lives with that kind of strength and courage!

CHAPTER 5

Who Is Your Child

_____

As we solidify who we are individually, as parents, and in our relationships with others, it becomes easier to see our children as separate and unique personalities rather than extensions or copies of ourselves.

Then we can give our children the best possible gift, which is knowing who they are and how they want to be in the world. We can begin to recognize, encourage, and support what makes them unique. This includes their personal preferences, beliefs, values, gifts, talents, passion, and purpose in life.

Behavioral scientists continue to research and debate the role of nature versus nurture in a child's development. Parents with multiple children often comment that they can clearly see how each child was born with his or her own unique temperament. With some children it is clear from the very beginning how they are going to take in and interact with the world. With others those patterns are discovered over time.

> **Our children are born with inherent gifts, but how we nurture our children has a tremendous influence on who they become.**

A child can have a talent allowing him to be a great musician, but if he's never exposed to music or musical instruments, that gift may go unnoticed or underdeveloped. She could have the potential to be a great athlete, but without sports equipment or good coaches, her skills would never be actualized. He could be the next Einstein or Bill Gates, but without great teachers or academic opportunities, his full potential may never be achieved.

If the home we create for our children is full of anger and dysfunction, that too affects who are children will become. Children who live in chaos or fear have to focus their energy on surviving. They do not have enough internal resources to fully self-actualize because the necessary support isn't in place. Although they may have been born with great potential, these children aren't given the opportunity to explore or develop their gifts, which often leaves them feeling inadequate, overwhelmed, anxious, frustrated, and angry. Some of these children can find other people, resources, or inspiration along the way so they can overcome their childhood deficits. Others just drift through life, constantly meeting with failure and acting out in unproductive and damaging ways.

So, what we do as parents does matter. It matters a lot, and it's up to us to find the strength, courage, and resources to empower our children to be the best they can be.

When it comes to discovering who our children are, often our role is that of a detective seeking out clues, an explorer charting new territories, or a reporter documenting an unfolding story. It is our job to assist our children in the process of self-discovery, help them grow in self-awareness, and help celebrate when they exhibit new levels of self-mastery.

As parents there are also times we are like the stone sculptor, chiseling away the rough edges of our children so their true beauty can emerge. It is an art (unfortunately not a hard science!) to develop just the right amount of pressure and gently eliminate the unnecessary pieces. Too little pressure and the rough edges remain. Too much pressure and the entire piece can crack and be ruined.

From the day your child is born, the process of discovery can begin. It's never too early or too late to start.

As your child changes and grows, you can watch for the following signs.

What makes your child unique? What are their interests? What holds their attention? What gets them excited? These are the seeds of discovering their passions in life. Knowing their passions can help lead them to discover their purpose and the ways in which they can contribute to society as adults.

As you observe your children with others their age, what do you see that's unique about their interests?

What is your child's temperament? Are they outgoing or shy? Are they introverted or extroverted? Are they a big thinker or great at focusing on the details? Do they decide things with the head or heart? Do your children like living with a schedule or prefer to go with the flow?

Are your children risk takers? Are they more physical or cerebral? Are they slow to warm or at home wherever they land?

Are your children overwhelmed by too much sensory input? Do you find the more stimulation they experience the happier they are, or does it depend on the circumstance and situation?

How do your children handle their emotions? Do they internalize what they feel? Is it hard to get a read on what's going on with your children? Instead of expressing do they act out when their feelings are intense? Are they highly expressive children? Are they constantly telling you about their shifts in moods and why they are feeling the way they are?

What kind of learners are your children? Are they visual learners who learn best from watching? Are they auditory learners who learn best from listening? Are they kinesthetic learners who learn best through movement and activity?

Everyone falls somewhere along the spectrum in these categories (and many others), and it is the unique combination of points along these lines that determines our true self. Some of the attributes are hardwired; some will shift over time.

It's important to be aware of where your child is for now and help order his or her life accordingly. When we ask children to live in a way that is counter to their temperament, we can create unnecessary and unwanted frustration for our children and ourselves.

What are your child's gifts and talents? Everyone is born with a unique set of gifts and talents which we develop along the way. (Again this is the nature versus nurture debate.) Do your children show interest in music, sports, nature, animals, building, inventing, dancing, drama, taking care of people, how the body works, or how the universe works? Do they seem to have an aptitude for science, math, writing, or history?

At some point along the way, children usually show an interest in nearly all of these things, but over time you may begin to see a pattern emerge. Perhaps there is a thread that weaves through all their interests or something they keep circling back to even as they try new things. If so you're probably beginning to determine their gifts and talents, and you can look for opportunities for your children to explore that aspect of themselves more deeply. Exposure to more chances to utilize the emerging gift or talent will help clarify if it's something significant or just a passing phase.

How will you know the difference? If it continues to hold their interest, brings them joy, and is something at which they are excelling and willing to put in the required effort to reach higher levels of participation, then chances are it is a natural gift or talent that will stay with them for quite some time.

The key, and we can't stress this enough, is that the talent is drawn out from within them. It cannot be something you are imposing on them. It's so easy to get caught up in the pride we feel, the time and money we've invested, and the hopes and dreams we've glimpsed at the possibility that their gifts or talents will bring them success in adulthood. So this is one area, as parents, we need to constantly keep ourselves in check. Otherwise, like the stone sculptor, a little too much pressure, and our masterpiece can crack.

What is your child's motivation? Finding what motivates our children is another important aspect in helping discover who they are. We know for sure an important aspect in successfully transitioning our children into adulthood is that they possess the ability to be internally rather than externally motivated.

In other words, be careful not to overdo it when it comes to standing over your children, rewarding them, or punishing them in an effort to motivate. If we get caught in the trap of externally motivating our children to think, act, or behave in a certain way, we might as well get used to supporting them throughout their lives because that's one of the fastest ways to sabotage their ability to make it on their own.

Helping to create a shift from external to internal motivation can be a challenge. If, for example, you know your child is underachieving at school, you can set up external rewards (such as money for good grades) or external consequences (such as taking away screen time). For some children that will be enough to decide internally they want to do better. For other children that just establishes a battle of wills because they feel their parents are trying to control them.

Also be aware that each time we do something for our children they are (or should be) capable of doing for themselves, we send the message that they aren't able to care for themselves. Human beings often learn more through their failures than their successes. If we give our children a chance to fail at the little things in life and find ways to overcome those disappointments, we allow them to realize they are capable of overcoming difficulties and being resilient when life throws them a curve.

When it comes to praising our children, research has shown that praising them for being smart, beautiful, talented, etc., actually undermines their internal motivation. By praising our kids for inborn attributes rather than for their effort or what they've accomplished, we're sending the message that they don't need to try or work at something in order to achieve.

What are your child's beliefs and values? As our children continue to grow, we will begin to see their beliefs and values exhibited through their behaviors. Sometimes they reflect ours. Sometimes they are searching for their own. (Aaah, the dreaded adolescent years!) While we wish we could just open the top of their heads and pour in what we would like, that isn't a real option.

We can, however, model our beliefs and values. We can talk with our kids about our family's standards and ideals. We can reinforce our children when we see them exhibiting principles we hold in high regard. We can also express our disappointment or point out the consequences of certain behaviors that go against what our family feels is important. By continually moving through these steps, we can help our children consciously choose a set of beliefs and values that will serve them well in life. We can help them choose ideals they won't compromise regardless of who they are with or what temptations are presented along the way.

What is your child's cultural background and family history? Just as we examined our own cultural background and family history, our children are the ones who will carry on or, in some cases, end our legacies. Often we think the story of our children's lives begins with chapter one, but in reality the stories of our lives, our parents' lives, and generations past are the prologue and beginning chapters of our children's book of life. It's important to share our traditions and history with our children so they understand where they come from and the good and bad aspects of what has preceded them.

Left unacknowledged and unspoken, the traditions we value may not be as clear to our children as we think. Therefore are children are less likely to embrace and carry those traditions forward into their adult lives and future families.

Similarly, left unacknowledged and unspoken, negative patterns can continue through our children's lives, which is something most of us would prefer not to happen. By bringing negative family patterns into the light, the chances of repeating similar circumstances can be lessened.

We want to pass healthy family traditions and histories to our children, but like a baton in a relay race, if we hold on too tight, the pass cannot be successfully made. We have to master the skill of placing the baton firmly in our children's hands and then letting go so they can take off and effectively run their leg of the race in their own unique style.

What are your child's personal dreams? The key to observing, documenting, and supporting our children's dreams is to keep the word "personal" constantly in our consciousness. It is *their* dreams we want to focus on. It is not us imposing our dreams for their lives onto them. Help your children dream by asking open-ended questions about the many possibilities in their lives.

It's not just about what they want to do. They can also dream about how they want to be. Does your child dream about living in a city or on a farm? If your family won the lottery, how would your child like to spend the money? If your child could snap his/her fingers and develop any talent, what would it be? Why?

Playing these kinds of "what if" games with your children can help you get a sense of what they dream for their lives. It can be a great game to play over dinner from time to time. Don't forget to also share the dreams you have for you and your family's life sometimes.

What are your child's short- and long-term goals? As you begin discovering who your children are and what makes them unique, then you can assist them in learning how to set both short- and long-term goals for themselves.

Again, notice the words "for themselves." As parents we're not setting the goals for them and then expecting them to follow through. We're engaging with them, teaching them how to break a big dream into manageable steps, and then setting achievable goals. It's a process and a skill that most successful people have developed, and it's a valuable tool to teach our kids.

We have provided an exercise to begin to capture some of the observations about the unique attributes your children possess. We suggest you update and review this exercise regularly so you can document what you're discovering and acknowledge patterns as you see them emerge.

As a word of caution while watching for clues about who your child is, avoid the temptation to label your child with those words. Observations are great, but attaching a label means you respond to or reference your child using those words.

Words have power, and when children exhibit certain behaviors, while they may be an indication of a permanent pattern in their lives, it can also simply be a passing phase. If we start to label and identify them with that behavior, talent, or gift, we may be doing them a disservice. We may be robbing them of the ability to feel good about their efforts, making them feel they need to stick with something even if it isn't right for them, or making them behave in a certain way in order to grow into the label they've been given.

Even seemingly harmless labels like "the quiet one," "the laid-back one," or "the funny one" can send a child a message that that is who he/she is and how he/she is expected to act in relation to others both inside and outside the family.

While we recommend you stay away from labeling of any kind, it's vitally important you avoid negative labels. Labeling a child "stupid," "slow," or "stubborn" gives the child the message that that is how you see him/her. It can take a lifetime (or a whole lot of therapy) for a child to get past negative childhood labels.

If you have more than one child, fill out the following exercises for each child separately.

Chapter Five of My Parent Handbook—
Who Is My Child

Who Is My Child (Becoming)

1. I find my child is most interested in...

2. Even though interests shift and change, a common thread I see is...

3. When I observe my child, I see he/she is more:

    a. outgoing/solitary

    b. structured/free-flowing

    c. analytical/creative

    d. organized/messy

e. sensitive/tough

f. auditory/visual/kinesthetic

g. risk taker/risk averse

h. experimental/results-oriented

i. comical/serious

j. physical/cerebral

4. When I think of what comes naturally to my child, I think of...

5. When I think of where my child tends to excel, I think of...

6. What I value most about my child is...

7. My child is motivated:

a. externally

b. internally

8. Does my child like pleasing:

    a. me

    b. teachers

    c. friends

    d. him/herself

9. I notice my child exhibiting which values and beliefs. (For example, I see he/she is honest, trustworthy, hardworking, empathetic, tolerant, willing to stand up for others, etc.)

10. I see my child carrying on positive family history and/or traditions such as...

11. I see my child carrying on unhealthy family history and/or traditions such as...

12. Because of my own observations and/or comments from teachers, neighbors, family members, and friends, I have concerns about...

13. In response to those concerns, I will...

14. My child's current hopes and dreams are to...

15. I see the following pieces are in place to help my child move toward his/her dream:

16. I would like to incorporate the following into my child's life to allow him/her to take steps toward his/her desired future:

17. The best parts of my child are...

18. This year I would like to teach my child...

19. This year it would be good if my child could...

20. It makes me so happy to see my child...

21. I need to tell my child more often that...

A Letter to My Child

Write a letter to your child expressing what you are feeling about who he/she is becoming. Add some words of wisdom, and include your hopes and dreams for him/her when appropriate. If writing this letter brings up negative emotions, use it as a tool to focus on what you can do over the next year to help create change. If it brings up positive emotions, consider sharing it with your child as a way to provide him/her with affirmation.

We'll talk about doing a regular review of all the exercises in this book. However, this is one we highly recommend doing on an annual basis. Be sure to keep a copy in your parent handbook. You may want to gift your children with an entire set of letters at a special milestone in their lives (e.g., becoming a teenager, turning sixteen, graduating, turning eighteen, starting college, getting married, expecting a child, etc.)

Dear...

Sometimes it takes real strength and courage to allow our children to be who they are, honor their uniqueness, support their dreams, and support them along their chosen paths. This is especially true if they are different than who or what we thought they would be.

Perhaps that's why they say being a parent is one of the most important yet toughest jobs we do!

CHAPTER 6

How Do You Match with Your Child

―――――――――

By now you have considered who you are as an individual, how you and your co-parent complement each other, how you fit with your extended family, friends, and community, and who you see your child being and becoming. It's wonderful and easy when many of those things match up, but what do you do when distinct differences between you and your child appear?

Knowledge is power.

> **Knowing how you are similar and different from your child can help you share each other's strengths and celebrate the differences.**

If we don't stop to notice and become aware of our similarities and differences, it's easy to fall into a pattern of thinking one way is right and the other is wrong. We may then start feeling responsible for changing or fixing the other person. This could be parents trying to change or fix kids when they are younger or kids, especially adolescents, trying to change or fix their parents.

One example of a common difference is when an extroverted parent has an introverted child. Extroverts are in the majority, and the world tends to be set up around their preferences. Social activities, school settings, and working environments often are more difficult for the introvert. It's not that introverts can't navigate these places, but they need time to be quiet or alone, recharge their batteries, and process their world. If an introverted child comes home from school and needs to be alone or quiet for a period of time, an extroverted parent might jump to the conclusion something is wrong or that the child is being antisocial.

If an extroverted parent understands the needs of an introverted child, however, the parent can ensure the child's life is structured in a way that provides him/her the time and space necessary to function at his/her best. This can be done without judging or making the child feel bad about the way he/she is wired. It's also an opportunity for the parent to see the world through the child's eyes and get a different perspective that can help in his/her own personal growth.

If we raise our children with the knowledge that each of us is unique, we all have value and important gifts to bring to the family, and it is in honoring our differences that we can grow, learn, and support each other, then there's no need to make one person right and the other wrong. There's no need to try to change or fix someone else.

If our children go out into the world with this knowledge, they will be more comfortable with who they are and far less likely to bow to peer pressure in order to fit in or please someone else. They will have been taught that everyone has value and differences are something to be celebrated. They will go out into the world with the strength of knowing they are OK just the way they are.

Children pick up these messages from their parents very early in life, so it's important to monitor the verbal and nonverbal, intended and unintended, and explicit and implicit messages we send on a regular basis.

The following exercise will help you examine the similarities you share and the differences you see between who you are and who your child is becoming. We suggest each parent fill it out independently, and then you can talk about what you're finding.

Chapter Six of My Parent Handbook—
How Well Do I Match with My Child

Assessing Myself

1. I find myself most interested in...

2. A common thread I see in all my interests is...

3. When I think about myself, I am more:

    a. outgoing/solitary

    b. structured/free-flowing

    c. analytical/creative

THE COURAGE TO PARENT

d. organized/messy

e. sensitive/tough

f. auditory/visual/kinesthetic

g. risk taker/risk averse

h. experimental/results-oriented

i. comical/serious

j. physical/cerebral

4. When I think of what comes naturally to me, I think of...

5. When I think of where I tend to excel, I think of...

6. The thing I value most about myself is...

7. Am I motivated externally or internally?

8. I most enjoy pleasing:

a. my family

b. my boss

c. my friends

d. myself

9. The beliefs and values I hold most dear are...

Now go back and compare your answers to the answers you gave for questions one through nine in the previous chapter.

Where do you line up? Where are you very different?

Can you find ways to relate to and celebrate the differences?

Are there differences that are hard for you to understand and support?

What are the messages (verbal and nonverbal, intended and unintended, and explicit and implicit) you are sending your children on a regular basis?

Note to Self

As I think about all the questions above, what do I need to remind myself to do or stop doing in order to be more accepting of my child, even in the areas where he/she is very different than me? This note is something I can reference when I feel frustrated or tempted to change my child.

Dear Me:

This year I need to remember...

It can be difficult to allow your children to be different than you. Somewhere we must be genetically wired to want our children to become the new and improved version of ourselves! However, we can't live our lives, correct the mistakes we made, or alleviate our regrets by forcing our children to follow in our footsteps.

Our children have the right to live their own lives, and as parents we're given the gift of the best seats in the house as they unfold and blossom into their very best selves.

CHAPTER 7

Preparing Your Child for Life

Our self-knowledge and self-awareness are like the rudder of a ship. A rudder can't calm the water or change the current or the waves, but it does give us the ability to set our course, steer our ship, and navigate through choppy, rough seas. Without a rudder our ship is at the mercy of the elements, which can blow us off course.

None of us would ever allow our children to set sail across the ocean without training, practice, and all the right equipment (including a good rudder). But how many of us stop to think about what training, practice, and equipment our children need to navigate through life?

As a parent we have to remember we're not raising kids. We're raising adults. We take them from newborns to babies to toddlers to preschoolers to kindergarteners to elementary school children to middle school students to teenagers to young adults starting college or a career to responsible, productive adults capable of caring for themselves and contributing to society!

It is our job is to prepare our children for the next stage of life.

If we don't stop to think about the skills and tools adults need to be responsible and productive members of society, how can we be confident we're preparing our children to step into that role? Also, how can we be frustrated or disappointed in our children's outcomes if we haven't provided them with the skills and tools they need? If we don't prepare our kids and ensure they have what they need to be ready to transition, who will prepare our kids for life?

Schools are in business to provide our children with an academic education. A hundred years ago parents sent their children to school to learn math, reading, and writing. These were skills agricultural parents didn't necessarily possess.

Schools are designed to educate. It's up to us, however, to prepare our kids for life. If we don't realize the importance of this aspect of parenting, we may send our kids into the world with a great academic education, but they will struggle without the emotional skills needed to manage life.

A person's level of emotional intelligence, even more so than IQ, can be a predictor of how well a person will do as he/she moves through life. So it is vital we ensure our children are given an opportunity to develop these skills.

What kinds of skills are we talking about?

Being self-aware and self-accepting. This is the foundation for developing self-esteem. We want to encourage our children to be involved in ongoing self-discovery and personal growth. This way they can successfully learn how to manage their physical and emotional well-being.

As children learn what they are good at, what makes them special, and how it is they operate best in the world, they can then begin to define what a meaningful life would look like for them. As they grow in the knowledge of what makes them unique, they can begin the process of accepting who they are. This ultimately allows them to live authentically and develop an ongoing commitment to the process we talked about previously.

Having empathy for others. Children who are self-aware and self-accepting are far more likely to develop a healthy sense of empathy for others. They become more compassionate and are able to tune into other people's feelings, seeing the world beyond just themselves. Empathy is an important trait as we move into adulthood because it's essential for developing strong, healthy personal and professional relationships.

Having the ability to make good decisions. We want to ensure our children have several decision-making models to utilize when big decisions need to be made. After all, children are faced with considerably more choices and options than past generations. It is vital they be given opportunities to make decisions at early ages so they can experience the consequences (good and bad) of their choices and learn what works and what doesn't. Decision-making is like a muscle that needs to be developed and strengthened. This way, as our children grow older and the consequences become more serious, they've put in the practice necessary to make that muscle strong.

In order to make the best decisions possible, children need to learn to question what's going on, see the options available, determine the short- and long-term consequences of their choices, and know what's important in their lives. Decision-making is a process, and in order to have the best possible outcomes, we have to work through all the steps. We must learn to be responsive rather than reactive as we move through life. As a parent we can't make decisions for our children, but we can model good decision-making, give them various tools, be there to celebrate their victories, and encourage them to pick themselves up when they're not happy with their results.

Knowing how to set and maintain healthy boundaries. Children learn about setting and maintaining boundaries by what they see modeled at home. What does it mean to set and maintain healthy boundaries? It's about knowing where you end and I start, what I am responsible for and what I am not, and what I can control and what I can't.

Boundaries determine how we will allow others to treat us and how we will interact with others. It's about knowing ourselves and honoring each other as individuals so we can fully be with another person without personally paying a cost.

Boundaries are about discipline, how we set them for ourselves and our children. Boundaries are about knowing when to stand firm and when to be flexible. They are about being consistent yet kind in our correction and follow-through.

When we set and maintain healthy boundaries, we are able to be with people empathetically but not take on their feelings or feel responsible for their outcomes. We learn how to take care of ourselves without expecting others to save or rescue us.

Being an effective communicator. Good communication plays an important role in all aspects of our lives. It plays into how we feel about ourselves, our relationships with others, and our success at school or work. Good communication is the foundation of trust in all relationships, and it helps us feel safe.

However, employers, colleges, and other schools are reporting that young people today do not communicate as effectively as in the past. It appears that as electronic communication is increasing, face-to-face communication is decreasing. For many of our young people, this is causing a deficit in skills. While e-mailing, Face-booking, tweeting, and other forms of social media certainly have a place in the world, young people cannot be totally dependent on those forms of communication. They do not convey the same level of tone, emotion, connection, or intimacy that face-to-face communication provides and that we, as human beings, need.

Electronics depersonalize communication, allowing boundaries to blur and providing a format to write things we would never say to a person's face.

While communication skills were once naturally developed through play, family dinners, intergenerational connections, and so on, we now need to be proactive in ensuring our children are developing good communication skills that will carry them through life.

Knowing how to deal with conflict. Conflict is a part of life because we are all unique, and we have differences. It's important our children understand that fact and develop skills to handle conflict when it presents itself. We can manage conflict by learning how to find common ground, accepting and celebrating differences, and knowing when to walk away from a situation or particular relationship.

Growing in self-awareness, self-acceptance, and self-confidence facilitates being able to handle conflict.

Being able to handle stress. Stress is at an all-time high, and it's getting worse. More than ever children need to be able to recognize and manage stress. Some people find exercise, downtime, hobbies, relationships, time in nature, etc., helps reduce stress levels.

Meditation is a great way to counter stress because it's often not our circumstances that cause stress but what we tell ourselves about the circumstances. Meditation helps us get control over all the mindless chatter most of us experience.

Quieting the internal interference. We all have "voices" in our heads. These are both positive and negative messages we have received from friends, family, and society. We need the tools to recognize and consciously choose which messages we're going to follow, and we need to learn to access the voice inside ourselves that represents who we truly are.

Being resilient. Children need to learn that whatever setbacks, failures, or unfortunate circumstances life happens to throw their way, they can survive, get up, move through it, and become stronger through the experience. If we always run interference for our children to prevent them from feeling uncomfortable, making mistakes, or failing, we rob them of the opportunity to develop this important quality.

Managing a twenty-first century lifestyle. The world is rapidly and constantly changing, and if we are going to survive and thrive in our twenty-first century existence, we need to consciously equip ourselves to deal with the following challenges:

Technology. This is taking over many people's lives. While it is a wonderful tool, it is something we need to learn to manage. Oftentimes technology can interfere with good communication skills, cause undue and unnecessary stress, and be highly addictive.

Rapid change. Thanks in part to the advances in technology, everything around us is rapidly changing. With change comes stress. It also brings a lot of uncertainty and unpredictability. Being able to manage change is a necessary skill for all of us.

Global society, diversity, relocation, and lack of extended family. With the development of a global society, we must be able to accept and respect diversity of other cultures. Because people move more often, we must be adaptable and resourceful as we learn to cope without extended family in place.

Chapter Seven of My Parent Handbook—
How Well Is My Child Prepared for Life?

Assessing My Child

Assessing how prepared our children are for life is clearly a function of their age and stage of development, but no matter what their age/stage, when assessing the skills needed to grow into adulthood, we are either planting the seeds, watching skills sprout, or seeing mastery in full bloom.

On each of the following skills, indicate whether you:

> N = realize seeds have **n**ot been planted

> S = see skills **s**prouting

> M = observe your child **m**astering the skills (at an age/stage appropriate level)

____ being self-aware and self-accepting

____ having empathy for others

____ having the ability to make good decisions

_____ knowing how to set and maintain healthy boundaries

_____ being an effective communicator

_____ knowing how to deal with conflict

_____ being able to handle stress

_____ quieting the internal interference

_____ being resilient

_____ managing twenty-first century lifestyles (including technology, diversity, etc.)

It takes strength and courage to prepare our children for life, and we're the ones they look to in order to learn these important skills.

CHAPTER 8

Building Your Skills

If we have strong emotional skills, we can pass them onto our children. Unfortunately, parents can't teach what they don't know.

If, as you read the previous chapter, you heard yourself saying, "I wish I had more of that," then you might want to consider developing a learning plan for yourself.

After all, the skills we have outlined are great building blocks all of us should possess, whether we're a parent or not. Maybe the desire to help our children be the best they can be motivates us to develop more skills ourselves, but those skills will help enhance our lives as an individual, friend, family member, and worker.

First do an honest assessment of your emotional skills, and determine your strengths and weaknesses.

You are your children's best and most powerful life coach.

Chapter Eight of My Parent Handbook—
Building My Skills

Assessing Myself

When thinking of your mastery of emotional skills, rate yourself in each area:

M = I feel I have **m**astered this skill

S = I am **s**omewhat competent in this area

N = I know I **n**eed improvement with this skill

____ being self-aware and self-accepting

____ having empathy for others

____ having the ability to make good decisions

____ knowing how to set and maintain healthy boundaries

____ being an effective communicator

____ knowing how to deal with conflict

____ being able to handle stress

____ quieting the internal interference

____ being resilient

____ managing twenty-first century lifestyles (including technology, diversity, etc.)

Now go back and compare your answers to how you responded for your child in the previous chapter. How do the ratings you gave yourself compare to those you gave your child? Is your child weak in the same areas? Do your strengths match? Where are you being a good role model of these skills for your child?

Celebrate where you've done a good job!

Enhancing My Skills

Take some time to think about what skills you would like to develop further. This can be for your own personal benefit or to be a better role model for your child. Prioritize the top three skills you'd like to start on right away.

There are books and classes to help you develop the skills you've identified, or you can choose to work with a coach or therapist to gain new skills. Pick the skill you want to start with, then mark your calendar for several weeks from now. List the other two skills you want to work on next. When you get to that week on your calendar, decide if you want to continue working on your first choice or if you're ready to move to the next.

Repeat this process as often as necessary to keep yourself on track in your learning and developmental process.

In order to fully integrate any new idea or skills, first we need to be aware of our desire to change. Next we need to grow in our knowledge of the options for change, and then we need to commit to practicing the change until it becomes a part of us. At that point we own it. That skill is ours for life.

The hard work is the practice. It's one thing to possess knowledge on a subject; it's quite another to master it. So we encourage you to hold yourself accountable, and celebrate your small steps and victories along the way! Log your successes in your parent handbook to track your growth along the way.

It takes strength and courage to stay the course, but if you master the emotional skills your children need to become productive, responsible adults, you will greatly enhance their chances of mastering those skills also. You are your children's best and most powerful life coach.

CHAPTER 9

Active Listening and Emotional Coaching

To ensure you develop a strong and lasting bond with your child, it's important to develop two additional skills: active listening and emotional coaching.

What do we mean by those terms?

An active listener is someone who doesn't just hear what someone is saying but is fully present to what's being said. With time constraints and the interference of technology, it's easy to be distracted and not fully listen to what our children are saying. Have you ever been driving, texting, working on the computer, or thinking about other things when your child was talking to you about something?

Have you ever had the experience when you think you had a conversation with someone, but the other person doesn't remember it, or someone reminds you of a conversation you had, but you have no recollection of that taking place?

Maybe you think you're engaged in a conversation but suddenly realize you didn't hear the last few sentences. Have you ever been watching a movie or TV show, engaging with the characters, and enjoying the plot only to realize your mind has wandered, and you've missed what was just said or happened? Thank goodness for DVRs! Unfortunately life happens in real time, and there is no rewind button for when we temporarily check out.

When we're fully present in the moment, we are more likely to engage in active listening. We can take in what's being said without thinking about the next question we're going to ask, ways to solve the problem being presented, or what we need to accomplish next week. We're just listening, and when it's appropriate, we speak.

It's an acquired skill for most of us, and even the best active listeners aren't necessarily in that mode all the time.

Another aspect of active listening is taking in the entirety of what's being communicated. While the words are important, people also express themselves through body language and the emotions they are attempting to express.

As an active listener, we are also sometimes playing the role of an emotional coach. We assist the other person in naming and expressing the feelings he/she is experiencing so that person can resolve the underlying issue.

Children need emotional coaches. They're experiencing all kinds of feelings and can become extremely frustrated and agitated when they don't know how to properly name and express them. Their brains are still developing, and they need help making sense of and integrating their day-to-day experiences.

The four basic keys to being an emotional coach to your child are:

- Acknowledge and process your own feelings in a healthy way.

- Have empathy for what your child is experiencing.

- Take your child's emotions seriously.

- Be willing to understand your child's perspective.

Acknowledge and process your own feelings in a healthy way. As is the case with active listening, emotional coaching is a skill to be learned and developed. It starts by learning how to acknowledge your own emotions and process them in a healthy way. If, when you're feeling frustrated or stressed, you blame everyone else, yell to release the tension, or storm off to pout because you feel like a victim, your child will see those options as acceptable behavior and may follow in your footsteps when similar emotions rise.

Feelings are not simply something we randomly experience. Feelings are clues to how we're interpreting what's going on in our lives. They are not something to be acted upon.

> **Feelings are an expression, just like words. They let us and those around us know what's going on in our lives.**

If we're angry, that's not permission to throw a fit or hurt someone in retaliation. Anger is just an indicator we are feeling threatened, dissatisfied, or unhappy.

If, however, we're afraid to acknowledge, experience, and work through the anger and ask ourselves what it is really about, we never get to the real issue causing us to be afraid, frustrated, or sad. We just walk around feeling angry a lot.

Have empathy for what your child is experiencing. It may not be a convenient time for your child to have a meltdown, especially if you've had a hard day, are out in public, or are with someone who already judges your ability to parent properly! But if you can empathize with the fact your child is feeling distress, and you have the potential to help, patience can truly be a virtue. The reason or intensity behind your child's emotion may not make sense to you, but if you can withhold judgment, resist being embarrassed, and support your child in processing what's going on, you are teaching him/her how to someday do that independently.

Take your child's emotions seriously. Again, what your child is feeling may not make sense to you. But if you can stop and realize that what he/she is feeling is real, legitimate, and perhaps the best way he/she knows how to express what's going on, then it's easier to take those emotions seriously and try to help. When your child is experiencing an extreme emotion, it's easy to say, "You shouldn't feel that way." But in dismissing the emotions as silly or wrong, you send the message you're not interested.

Be willing to understand your child's perspective. We see the world through adult eyes, but our children's brains aren't fully developed, and they see the world from a child's point of view. As an emotional coach for our children, we need to step back and try to see the world from their perspective. In doing so we can help expand their way of looking at a situation or person and broaden their perspective, which can serve them well the next time they find themselves in a similar situation.

Some of these suggestions may seem awkward, but with practice you'll find your own style, and these skills can become second nature to you.

There are a myriad of feelings a person can experience. The more we are able to name and give voice to our internal sensors, the easier we can express and deal with what's behind those feelings.

The greater your emotional vocabulary and the ease with which you can name and express what's going on within you, the more you will be able to help your child do the same.

Take a look at the following word chart and think about the emotions you experience in an average day, week, or month and how you express and work through what you're feeling.

Emotional Vocabulary

Using the feeling words below, indicate whether they are an expression of being ANGRY (A), HAPPY (H), SAD (S), or SCARED (SC):

aggravated	elated
agitated	embarrassed
annoyed	encouraged
anxious	enthusiastic
apprehensive	enraged
blue	frantic
cheerful	frightened
contented	frustrated
delighted	furious
disappointed	gratified
discouraged	grieving
dissatisfied	great
ecstatic	gloomy

guilty	panicky
happy	peaceful
hate	peeved
helpless	relieved
hopeful	resentful
hopeless	tense
hostile	terrified
hurt	thankful
incensed	timid
infuriated	uneasy
intimidated	unhappy
irritated	vulnerable
joyful	worried
jubilant	wronged
love	
miserable	
mournful	

Why is it so important to name and express our feelings?

Can you picture what happens if children never learn this skill? What happens when they're seven? Or eleven? Or seventeen? Rather than acknowledging, expressing, and working through whatever they're experiencing in life, they act out. They are out of control, and deep down inside they want someone to help them figure out how to regain it, because it doesn't feel good when you think you have no control over your feelings, impulses, or actions.

Teenagers don't just wake up one day and decide they're going to get bad grades, start using alcohol/drugs on a regular basis, scream and yell at their parents, demand the world bend to their will, or be destructive to property or other people. Those kinds of behaviors are usually the result of unresolved feelings and experiences that have taken place over long periods of their short lives.

Knowing that our children's brains are growing and developing just like the other parts of their body offers us a greater understanding of why they are behaving the way they do. It's important to keep in mind that higher level reasoning skills aren't fully developed until a person is in his or her early twenties, which explains a lot about adolescent behavior!

To help our children learn to process their emotions, make sense of their experiences, and develop their higher level thinking skills, we need to utilize the following steps:

- **Be aware** of your own feelings and your child's.

- **Connect** on an emotional level.

- **Listen** with your active listening skills.

- **Name your emotions**, and help your children name and honor what they're feeling.

- **Engage in higher level reasoning processes**. Once the situation is calm, help your child reflect on the experience that triggered the emotions. Apply logic, ask questions, learn, and teach lessons.

How we handle this process, both for ourselves and our kids, directly influences how well our children will be able to express and deal with their emotions growing up and into adulthood. It's another acquired skill and one we need to teach them.

Here are a few exercises to help you assess and develop your skills in both active listening and being an emotional coach for your child.

Chapter Nine of My Parent Handbook—
Active Listening and Emotional Coaching

Active Listening

As the old saying goes, there is a reason we have two ears and only one mouth.

1. What percentage of time do you spend telling people what you are thinking and/or feeling? What percentage of time do you spend listening to what the person you are with is thinking and/or feeling?

2. How comfortable are you with silence, both by yourself and when talking with others?

3. How often do you spend time listening to your inner voice (the small whispers, your true self, the fears and concerns vying for your attention, etc.)?

4. How comfortable are you making eye contact with the person you're talking to?

5. Do you and your child make eye contact when talking?

6. Do you maintain an open, relaxed posture when talking with your children, even in uncomfortable situations and conversations?

7. When you're talking with people, how do you feel if they're not fully listening to you (i.e., they're distracted, taking phone calls, texting, or uninterested in what you're saying)?

8. What gestures do you tend to use to let someone know you're truly listening (nods, smiles, etc.)?

9. Do you use words to provide feedback to the person you are listening to (e.g., so you're thinking, so you're feeling, so you're saying, etc.)?

10. Can you defer judgment when someone is talking, or do you tend to jump in and assume what he/she is going to say?

THE COURAGE TO PARENT

11. How comfortable are you talking with people whose views are different than your own? Can you defer judgment in these kinds of situations?

12. Are you respectful in conversations with your children?

13. How effectively do you apply active listening skills:

    a. professionally

    b. with friends

    c. with family

    d. with your co-parent

    e. with your child

14. How might improving your active listening skills improve your relationships?

15. What are some ways you can improve your active listening skills? What would you like to focus on over the next few weeks?

Emotional Coaching

As you think about what it takes to be an emotional coach for your child, think about the following.

1. How comfortable are you expressing emotions and/or being with others when they are expressing theirs?

2. How well do you name your own emotions?

3. Do you share your emotions with your child?

4. On a scale from one to ten (one being the lowest), how comfortable are you connecting with people on an emotional level?

5. Do you take your child's emotions seriously? Do you spend time talking about your child's emotions, or do you tend to dismiss them?

6. Do your children use nonverbal clues about what they're feeling? (For example, if they're upset, does their activity level increase or decrease? Do they shut down or start behaving irrationally?)

7. One a scale from one to ten, where are your active listening skills?

8. Can you listen to your child without giving advice?

9. How comfortable are you with helping your child name his/her emotions?

10. Do you tend to tell your children how they "ought" to feel?

11. On a scale from one to ten, how comfortable are you helping your children "debrief" situations so they can make sense of what they are feeling and learn how to handle difficult situations or experiences?

12. On a scale from one to ten, how comfortable are you helping your children think through possible solutions and/or different outcomes when they have a problem with somebody?

13. On a scale from one to ten, how comfortable are you encouraging emotional expression and still setting limits on behavior (e.g., telling your child it's OK to feel, but it's not OK to act on the feeling)?

14. On a scale from one to ten, how comfortable are you helping your children draw their own conclusions, take away possible lessons from situations, and practice their higher level reasoning skills?

Note to Self

In order to be a more active listener and emotional coach for my child:

I would like to develop my ability to…

I will gain new information by…

In order to help me integrate these new skills, I will…

It takes strength and courage to commit to learning these skills, and it takes even more to stay with it when it gets tough. But practice makes perfect. Rare is the person who can actively listen and act as an emotional coach 100 percent of the time, but the more we hone and utilize these skills, especially when our children are distressed, the more confident we can be they will go out into the world and deal with whatever comes their way.

CHAPTER 10

Flexibility, Creativity, and Change

———————————

We don't want to mislead you. Being a parent and raising wonderful, well-adjusted kids isn't as easy as it is to write about. We do know, though, that if you are intentional, know what's nonnegotiable during the parenting process, acknowledge where you can be flexible and creative, and get comfortable managing change, it will go a long way in making the process a bit smoother.

> **When a tried-and-true approach with your child stops working, remaining flexible can help you find creative solutions that will.**

Flexibility is another vital skill every parent needs. Flexibility fuels creativity.

We know children go through stages in life, but it's important to remember they also go through phases. These are times when they have intense preferences for specific behaviors, playing with certain toys, participating in favored activities, or having a taste for particular foods.

When phases involve preferences we're not particularly fond of, they can be trying. When the phase has some positive aspects, it can be a great experience. For a period of time, we can predict what will make our child happy and respond accordingly.

However, transitioning from one phase to another can be difficult, and it is a perfect example of when flexibility and creativity can help you keep your sanity and perspective intact. Have you ever had a child in a banana eating phase? It's healthy, relatively inexpensive, and easy to pick up several bunches each time you're at the store, but when that phase suddenly passes, and you find yourself with three pounds of rotting bananas on your countertop, frustration can set in. If you remain flexible and allow your creativity to flow, a pile of rotten bananas can easily be turned into some loaves of banana bread, which you can share with friends, neighbors, or someone you keep meaning to thank for being in your life.

OK, maybe you're not a baker, and you'd just as soon throw the rotting bananas in the trash! The point is there are going to be times (many times) when we're inconvenienced, baffled, or frustrated by our child's behavior (or sudden shift in behavior). If you can remain flexible, though, and make room for the creative juices to flow, solutions you might not have otherwise thought of can be discovered. This allows you to be more responsive to your child's needs and more adaptable to change.

As a parent some things are nonnegotiable. Children need to be protected from injury, family rules need to be followed, and boundaries need to be honored. We should not compromise our beliefs and values, but how we go about protecting our children, what the family rules should be, and where the boundary lines are drawn evolve and change according to the child's age and development.

If we remain steadfast and insist we protect a ten-year-old in the same way we protect a one-year-old, insist a thirteen-year-old have the same boundaries as a three-year-old, or insist a sixteen-year-old follow the exact rules as a six-year-old, there are guaranteed to be problems!

When your child is toddling and exploring the world, discovering independence, and often meeting danger at every turn, we know how to childproof the world. Cabinet locks, baby gates, and electrical outlet plug covers are installed to protect your child during these explorations.

By the time that child turns twelve, all the childproof gear has disappeared, but the exploration of the world and quest for independence hasn't. Unfortunately this time a trip to the hardware store isn't going to offer what we need to have peace of mind that we've made the world safe. But if we've laid down the groundwork and built a relationship of trust through the years, that child will be more open to our words of caution and more willing to seek our advice.

Ask yourself, are you the same person you were ten or twenty years ago? Have you grown in your level of self-awareness, self-discipline, and self-acceptance? We hope so. Given the proper structure and opportunities, your child will also continue to develop and grow each and every year.

Parents need to grow and adapt (and often be very creative!) to meet children's needs because, as the old adage goes, the only constant in life is change.

Change is something with which many people aren't comfortable. It can be stressful. It can require us to learn things we really don't want to have to learn. It can feel overwhelming and never-ending like standing on shifting sand rather than steady ground, but sometimes all we need is a little time to help us manage change. We need time to regroup, reflect on why we're uncomfortable, and reorganize to meet the challenge.

The more we discover who we are and integrate all we have come to know into our daily lives, the more we can tolerate change. We know that, while the circumstances around us might be different, who we are on the inside will remain consistent. When we know who we are and what's important to our lives, we enhance our ability to make decisions that serve us well. We're less likely to have knee-jerk reactions to situations, and we become more measured and responsive in our choices.

Therefore, when change occurs we can figure out ways to navigate through it, and we can trust that, while our external circumstances may be changing rapidly, our internal knowledge and guidance remains steadfast.

Chapter Ten of My Parent Handbook—
Flexibility, Creativity, and Change

Flexibility, Creativity, and Change

1. How comfortable are you when plans, goals, deadlines, or preferred outcomes need to shift?

2. On a scale from one to ten (one being the lowest), how comfortable are you going with the flow in various areas of your life?

   a. personally

   b. professionally

   c. with your family

   d. when it comes to free/recreational time

3. On a scale from one to ten, how much do you enjoy finding creative solutions to issues or problems in various areas of your life?

    a. personally

    b. professionally

    c. in relationships

    d. at home

    e. with your children's stages of life

4. What's your reaction to the phrase, "change is the one constant in life"? What causes you the greatest concern when it comes to change?

5. When thinking about the famous saying, "Grant me the serenity to accept the things I cannot change, the courage to change the things I can, and the wisdom to know the difference," what comes to mind?

Note to Self

I want to remember that...

When it comes to being flexible and creative and managing change, I...

I want to celebrate my ability to..., or I want to enhance my ability to...

It takes courage to be focused, remain flexible, be creative, and manage change throughout life, but if we don't develop and hone those skills, how can we ever expect our children to be able to do so?

CHAPTER 11

Letting Go

———————————

My child is going out into the world without me!

Rarely is there a parent who doesn't experience the terror of these moments. Maybe it's the first time you leave your child with a babysitter or childcare provider or drop him/her off at the first day of preschool. Maybe it's when your child gets on the school bus for the first time, has that first sleepover at a friend's house, or goes off to overnight camp. Maybe it's when he/she goes to the movies with no adult supervision, attends his/her first dance with a group of friends, or has his/her first date. Maybe it's when he/she pulls out of the driveway without you in the car, goes off to college, or leaves your state to start a career. Whatever the circumstance, it's hard to let go.

The moment they place that newborn baby into our arms, our lives are forever changed. Suddenly there is another human being in this world whose life matters more than our own. That little baby is totally and completely dependent on us for sustenance and well-being. Left on his/her own, the child cannot survive. So what makes these kids think they can now as they go out into the world without us!

We invest so much of our time, energy, resources, and love into our children. We spend so much time nurturing that eternal bond, helping them feel attached to us, keeping them safe, and developing their trust, and then, on some appointed day, we're supposed to turn them loose and let them wing it on their own?

THE COURAGE TO PARENT

Letting go is never easy, but if we prepare our children to handle whatever stage of life they're about to enter, we can at least comfort ourselves knowing we've given them the skills, information, tools, and confidence to take the next step in their lives. If we do that at each and every stage, watching them succeed and celebrating their well-earned freedom along the way, then the letting go process can be a little less daunting.

If we hold too tight for too long, we rob our children of the chance to experiment with being independent and responsible in both small and big ways. We take away the opportunity for them to occasionally make mistakes and then discover they can survive setbacks. In moving forward, even in the face of defeat, children learn they are resilient enough to overcome whatever life sends their way.

Have you ever heard stories about parents who micromanage every aspect of their children's lives all the way through high school graduation? These parents then send their young adults off to college and are surprised when they go wild partying, skipping classes, and eventually dropping out because they don't know how to manage their freedom.

When parents hold on too tight, we send the message that our children aren't competent enough to manage their lives, so we must step in and do it for them. When we parent from fear, we make our children's worlds smaller. Sometimes that world becomes so small they aren't able to handle the day-to-day requirements needed to successfully transition into adulthood.

The letting go process is probably one of the toughest to master.

The amount of responsibility and freedom we were given in our lives and how well we handled it can impact our comfort level in letting our children go. If we haven't given our children the skills we've discussed throughout this book, then it's really hard to let them go. Instinctively we know they're not prepared to step out on their own.

The seeds of responsibility are planted early and need to be nurtured along the way. The tools and skills for being a responsible and productive young adult don't just spring forth when a child turns eighteen.

If we allow our four-year-old to help with meal preparation by setting the table or cleaning up afterward, and we allow his/her skills to grow, then our fourteen-year-old will be capable of preparing a meal and doing the dishes.

If we allow our five-year-old to pick out which outfit to wear to school, the child experiences what it's like to make decisions and experience the consequences of what is chosen. Then if we allow the child to practice with bigger decisions as they grow, as a fifteen-year-old, he/she is much more capable of making sound decisions.

If our six-year-old is taken to the store and given fifteen dollars to choose a birthday present for a friend's party, then, given additional allowances and responsibilities for managing a budget each year, at sixteen that child will have a much better sense of how to value and handle money.

Just like a strong oak tree, children need to be nurtured and pruned to survive the occasional storm and grow into full maturity. Mild winds on a sapling force the roots to go deeper to provide more stability, but too much wind can damage it. A seasoned gardener knows when to give the young tree space and when to give it a little extra protection. As a parent we're continually trying to find that wisdom.

Letting go can also trigger grief in parents. When our children move into a new phase of life, it means they're changing and growing up. Our role as their parent is shifting. They need us a little less. It can be particularly difficult if we have really enjoyed their current stage of life and aren't ready for it to be over.

This is a time when we need to be keenly aware of our feelings, work through them, and keep our focus on what's best for our children, even if it's hard for us. We don't want to hold our children back, but our emotions can definitely override our intellect when it comes to letting go.

There's also the complication that each child grows and matures at his or her own pace. Each has a different level of mastery of the skills discussed throughout this book. Each has a distinct temperament and personality that can greatly influence the direction that child needs/wants to go. When it comes to letting go, what works for one child might not work for another, even within the same family.

So how do we know if/when our children are ready for the next level? How do we know if we've given them the skills they need? How do we determine what they've mastered and what they're still struggling with? How do we know when our history or cultural background is getting in the way of allowing our children to thrive?

- **Pay** attention to the next phase for which that child needs to be prepared.

- **Remember** to ask questions to determine if that child is ready.

- **Evaluate** how well the child handles each level of responsibility and the freedom that goes with it.

- **Prepare** yourself for the letting go process. Figure out what you may need to let go of for the child to soar.

Always remember, the real joy of parenting comes in witnessing our children claim their victories and celebrating their successes when we see the good choices they are making in their lives.

Chapter Eleven of My Parent Handbook—
Letting Go

Letting Go

1. At what stage of life is your child?

2. As you think about the next stage of your child's life, what kinds of freedom and responsibility is he/she prepared to take on?

3. How can you prepare your child to handle freedom and take responsibility in the next stage?

4. What might you need to deal with in order to let go enough for your child to move forward?

5. The letting go process sometimes triggers a certain amount of sadness for parents. How can you work

through any sad feelings you have about your child growing up and becoming a bit more independent?

6. As you look back to your child's current or next stage of life, consider what your life was like when you were that age. Were they happy times for you? Did you meet developmental milestones? Did you have trauma during that time? Did your parents hold on too tight? How might your life experience be impacting how you parent now?

7. What will happen to your child's development if you don't become comfortable with the letting go process?

8. How can you celebrate (independently and/or with your child) as he/she grows in freedom, responsibility, and independence?

9. On a scale from one to ten (one being the lowest), how comfortable are you with letting go at this stage of your child's life?

10. Share your responses with your co-parent to see how you can compare, complement, and/or support each other with this process.

Note to World

My child is ready to take the next step toward being in the world on his/her own...

I am feeling...

I am being responsible...

I can celebrate...

The letting go process is hard at any age. However, the more we develop the skills discussed throughout this book, both for ourselves and our children, the greater confidence we will feel as they reach each milestone. In that way, while we may always feel a little bit of sadness that they're growing up too quickly and trepidation that they're going to make a mistake, we can relax a bit and better enjoy the process.

CHAPTER 12

Putting It All Together, Assessing Where You Are, and Looking Ahead

———————————

We hope the overview and approach we have presented in this book give you a clearer picture of the many components needed to help your children grow into productive, responsible adults.

We also hope that, by answering the questions in all the exercises, you have created a parent handbook that will provide you clarity and confidence as you move forward in your parenting process. Remember, you may not have all the answers at every turn, or you may still find difficulties with a particular child because of issues beyond the scope of this book, but you will at least have peace of mind knowing you did the work and were the best parent you could be.

We like to think of the parenting process as a whole person approach. As we parent we need to stay attentive to our child's physical, academic, and emotional development. (Depending on your belief system, a spiritual component might be present as well.) It's so easy to get caught up in how well our child is doing in school, in sports, or with other aspects of his/her personality and we can forget about the totality of what a child needs as he/she grows into adulthood.

Oftentimes the emotional component is overlooked, yet it is a vital piece of the puzzle. We've seen successful athletes, artistic geniuses, business people, politicians, and others in the public eye who have accomplished much because of a talent or gift, yet they have stumbled, crashed, and burned because they didn't have a strong emotional skill set.

The most successful parents know who they are, what's important to them, and how to equip themselves with the skills they must pass along to their children. They prepare themselves to be consistent role models for their children. They have the courage to do the work.

Nobody said it was easy, especially if you didn't have a great set of role models while growing up, or you weren't given the chance to develop the emotional skills you want to pass on to your kids.

But you'll increase your chance of parenting success and the chance of your child growing into a responsible, productive adult if you know:

- what's important to you and who you are as a person

- that you're on the same page with your co-parent, can compromise, and present a united front

- who your child is and what makes him/her unique

- how you match up with your child, how you can share your strengths, and how you can celebrate the differences

- what emotional skills your child needs to be prepared for life

- how to build your own skills so you can pass them on to your children

- that you can be a good role model and emotional coach for your child

- how to focus, be intentional, flexible, and developmentally appropriate with your child, and confident you can manage change

- that it is OK (in fact important) to let go as your child grows and develops

The thoughts you have captured in your parent handbook will help you remember what's really important during the parenting process. This way you don't waste precious moments in your child's life worrying about the small stuff.

Earlier in the book we also talked about the importance of assessing where you and your child are on a regular basis.

> **Periodically (at least annually) complete the following assessment, and think about what's next both in your development and in your child's.**

Log your assessments into your parent handbook each time. Maybe add a current picture of your child to remind you how much he/she has grown and changed since your last assessment.

Go back through your parent handbook and review all your entries. How do they compare to what you've answered in this assessment? Have you met the goals you previously set out for yourself? Have major changes taken place? Do you see big changes on the horizon?

If there have been some major shifts since the last time you did the exercises in this book, consider revisiting one or more of the chapters, and do the exercises again. You can continue to hone and expand your parent handbook throughout the parenting process.

Chapter Twelve of My Parent Handbook— Ongoing Assessments

Assessment

Today's date:

Think about the following questions for where you are today. The next time you do this exercise your answers may be the same, slightly changed, or completely different.

1. How do you feel about your ability to parent intentionally during this stage of your child's development?

2. What's important to you, and who are you as a person? What gives your life meaning and purpose? How do you measure how well you're living your life?

3. When you think about the questions above, are you and your co-parent on the same page? Where can you compromise? Where do you need to commit to presenting a united front?

4. What other people play an important part in your child's life? Are they good role models for your child? Are there discussions needed or new boundaries to be set in order to serve your child's best interests?

5. Who is your child, and what makes him/her unique? What qualities, talents, gifts, tendencies, personality traits, etc., are you seeing emerge from your child at this moment? (Is it time to write another "Letter to My Child" as suggested in chapter four?)

6. How do you match up with your child, and how can you share your strengths and celebrate your differences?

7. How comfortable are you with the changes taking place in both you and your child's lives?

8. Have there been any observations and/or comments from teachers, neighbors, family members, or friends that cause you to have concerns about your child?

9. What do you want to do in response to those concerns?

10. What emotional skills do you want to help your child develop so he/she can be better prepared for adulthood?

11. What emotional skills do you want to build for yourself so you can pass them on to your children?

12. Do you feel you are being a good role model and emotional coach for your child?

13. Do you feel you are comfortable with being flexible and developmentally appropriate with the expectations you have for your child?

14. On a scale from one to ten (one being the lowest), how comfortable are you with the letting go process as your child enters his/her next stage of development?

Note to Self

After doing this review, I see a lot of positive growth in myself and my child such as…

I would like to work on…

I want to go back and redo the exercises in chapter(s)…

I want to learn more about…

I want to celebrate…

I will mark my calendar to do a review again…

Congratulations! Not only have you created your very own parent handbook, but you are using it and integrating it into your parenting process.

It is our wish it will serve you and your child well for years to come.

References and/or Recommended Reading

Introduction and Chapter 1—Why Courage Is Vital to the Parenting Process

Dreikurs, Rudolf. *Children: The Challenge*. New York: Penguin Books, 1990.

Chapter 2—Intentional Parenting and Being a Positive Role Model

Covey, Stephen. *The 7 Habits of Highly Effective People*. New York: Free Press, 1989.

Chapter 3—What's Important to You

Seligman, Martin E.P. *What You Can Change and What You Can't: The Complete Guide to Successful Self-Improvement*. New York: Vintage Books, 2007.

Chapter 4—Are You on the Same Page

Walsh, David. *No: Why Kids—of All Ages—Need to Hear It and Ways Parents Can Say It*. New York: Free Press, 2007.

Chapter 5—Who Is Your Child

Brazelton, T. Berry, and Joshua D. Sparrow. *Touchpoints: Birth to Three*. Boston: Da Capo Press, 2006.

Brazelton, T. Berry, and Joshua D. Sparrow. *Touchpoints: 3 to 6*. Boston: Perseus Book Group, 2002.

Gold, Claudia M. *Keeping Your Child in Mind*. Boston: Da Capo Press, 2011.

Kaplan, Louise J. *Oneness and Separateness: From Infant to Individual*. New York: Touchstone, 1978.

On the Internet:

http://www.brazeltontouchpoints.org/

The vision of the Brazelton Touchpoints Center® is to ensure that all children grow up to become adults who can cope with adversity, strengthen their communities, engage as active participants in civic life, steward our fragile planet's limited resources, and nurture the next generation to be prepared to do the same.

Chapter 6—How Do You Match with Your Child

Hartzell, Mary, and Daniel J. Siegel. *Parenting From the Inside Out: How a Deeper Self-Understanding Can Help You Raise Children Who Thrive*. New York: Penguin Group, 2004.

Jacobson, Tamar. *"Don't Get So Upset!": Help Young Children Manage Their Feelings by Understanding Your Own*. Minnesota: Redleaf Press, 2008.

Chapman, Gary, and Ross Campbell. *The Five Languages of Love of Children*. Illinois: Moody Publishers, February 2012.

Chapter 7—Preparing Your Child for Life

Young-Eisendrath, Polly. *The Self-Esteem Trap: Raising Confident and Compassionate Kids in an Age of Self-Importance*. New York: Little, Brown and Company, 2008.

Goleman, Daniel. *Emotional Intelligence: 10th Anniversary Edition; Why It Can Matter More Than IQ*. New York: Bantam Bell, 2006.

Medina, John. *Brain Rules for Baby: How to Raise a Smart and Happy Child from Zero to Five*. Washington: Pear Press, 2010.

On the Internet:

http://www.search-institute.org/

The Search Institute's mission is to provide catalytic leadership, breakthrough knowledge, and innovative resources to advance the health of children, youth, families, and communities.

Chapter 8—Building Your Skills

Clark, Lynn. *SOS: Help for Parents: A Practical Guide for Handling Common Everyday Behavior Problems*. 3rd ed. Kentucky: SOS Programs & Parents Press, 2008.

Donovan, Denis, and Deborah McIntyre. *What Did I Just Say!?!: How New Insights into Childhood Thinking Can Help You Communicate More Effectively with Your Child*. New York: Henry Holt and Company, 1999.

Wolf, Anthony E. *Get Out of My Life, but First Could You Drive Me and Cheryl to the Mall?: A Parent's Guide to the New Teenager*. Canada: HarperCollins, 1999.

Chapter 9—Active Listening and Emotional Coaching

Gottman, John. *Raising an Emotionally Intelligent Child: The Heart of Parenting*. New York: Simon and Schuster Paperbacks, 1997.

Novick, Kerry Kelly, and Jack Novick. *Emotional Muscle: Strong Parents, Strong Children*. United States: Xlibris Corporation, 2010.

Faber, Adele, and Elaine Mazlish. *How to Talk So Kids Will Listen & Listen So Kids Will Talk*. New York: Scribner, 1980.

Siegel, Daniel, and Tina Payne Bryson. *The Whole-Brain Child: 12 Revolutionary Strategies to Nurture Your Child's Developing Mind, Survive Everyday Parenting Struggles, and Help Your Family Thrive*. New York: Delacorte Press, 2011.

On the Internet:

http://www.talaris.org

Talaris was founded in 2000 with the mission of supporting parents and caregivers in raising socially and emotionally healthy children.

Chapter 11—Letting Go

Coburn, Karen Levin, and Madge Lawrence Treeger. *Letting Go: A Parents' Guide to Understanding the College Years*. New York: HarperCollins Publishers, Inc., 2003.

Viorst, Judith. *Necessary Losses*. New York: Simon and Schuster, 1998.

Share Your Stories with Us

Now we want you to share your stories with us. During the parenting process, when have you been courageous in both big and small ways? What were your defining moments when you knew you had to stand strong, dig deep inside yourself, or seek outside help to get through a situation, phase, or issue?

How did you gain the skills, information, tools, and support you needed to get through that moment?

What did you discover about yourself? About different ways to parent? About your child?

We want to hear about your experiences. What have you learned during the parenting process you didn't expect? How might your story help or serve as an inspiration to another parent?

If you have stories about how something in this book helped or changed your parenting process or your child, we'd love to hear those stories too.

We might even be able to share them with others in another book.

So e-mail us and let us know!

Jan and Rosemary

www.TheCourageToParent.com

PS We also provide workshops to help parents work through many of the concepts in this book. If your school, organization, or group is interested, visit our website for more information.

Please limit all submissions to 1500 words or less. In making a submission, please know it might be shared with others. If you prefer to remain anonymous, just tell us when you submit.

Made in the USA
Charleston, SC
30 September 2012